365

Ways to

DEVELOP YOUR CHILD'S VALUES

CHERI FULLER

P.O. Box 35007, Colorado Springs, Colorado 80935

© 1994 by Cheri Fuller

All rights reserved. No part of this publication may be reproduced in any form without written permission from Piñon Press, P. O. Box 35007, Colorado Springs, CO 80935.

Library of Congress Catalog Card Number: 94-67030

ISBN 08910-98569

Cover illustration: Bob Fuller

Printed in the United States of America

Published in association with the literary agency of Alive Communications, P.O. Box 49068, Colorado Springs, CO 80949.

To Justin Oliver Fuller

There are little eyes upon you,
And they are watching night and day;
There are little ears that quickly
Take in every word you say.

There are little hands all eager
To do everything you do;
And a little child who's dreaming
Of the day he'll be like you.

You're the little sweetheart's idol;
You're the wisest of the wise;
In his little mind, about you
No suspicions ever rise.

He believes in you devotedly;
Holds that all you say and do,
He will say and do in your way
When he's grown up just like you.

There's a wide-eyed little sweetheart
Who believes you're always right;
And his ears are always open,
And he watches day and night.

You are setting an example
Every day in all you do;
For the little child who's waiting
To grow up to be like you.

—Anonymous

A Note to Parents

Responsibility, honesty, kindness, cooperation, determination—these and other values influence how your child will behave in the classroom, what kind of actions (ethical or unethical) he'll show on the playing field, in his career, and in social situations. And although values may be taught at school, home is still the best place to begin learning ethics and values.

"If children are to survive and thrive in this society," says Thomas Lickona, Ph.D., professor of education at the State University of New York, "it's up to parents to reclaim their authority and instill good values in their children at a very early age."[1] From the cradle throughout adolescence, childhood is the golden opportunity to instill a sense of conscience in our sons and daughters, a sense of right and wrong. The basic concepts of honesty, perseverance, hospitality, and respect for others can be worked into our everyday routines. They are best transferred through daily life rather than studying a workbook on values. Character-building is a day-by-day process, not taught overnight but by continual modeling, patient instruction, and family traditions and relationships.

Children observe their parents all the time—in the car, at the dinner table, in front of the television set. This is where they learn the most, because values are better "caught" than "taught." Our behavior and actions communicate a great deal about what is important to us, and our kids tend to follow in our footsteps. The transferring of values takes time and happens best in family togetherness—through the close, loving relationship between you and your child, through family rituals and traditions.

But what are our values based on? Rabbi and author Neil Kurshan says, "When we begin to doubt the absolute goodness of God, or even His very existence, we are left with only ourselves as the final arbiters of morality."[2] When that happens, when all morals are relative, children are left without firm values. Then he says they become confused and anxious over the array of alternatives.

Ethics means a universal, unchanging standard for behavior—standards that are above our own personal opinions and feelings of what's right and wrong, standards that don't change just because teenagers or business people loosen their behavior.[3]

Educators and sociologists say there is a crisis of values in the United States, particularly in young people. Thousands of children and teenagers seem devoid of conscience. Since every society and culture depends "directly on individuals who will act with integrity, and keeping the law, respecting life and property, loving one's family . . . helping the poor, paying taxes—all these depend on individual virtues like courage, duty, loyalty, charity, compassion and civility"[4]—it appears that we, and they, are in trouble unless we pick up the responsibility to impart character and values. The character of our children will in great measure determine the future, and the best place for them to begin learning enduring values is at home.

My hope is that these "365 ways" will help you instill solid values in your child. As you read this book, sit down and think, "What do I want to see grow in my child— what character qualities and values?" Let me encourage you that if you get only 1 percent growth in your child's character each week, you will see 50 percent growth in a year.[5] Little by little, as you get ready for your day, take your children to school and sports, have meals together, discuss things, talk and play together, and read bedtime stories, incorporating some of these 365 ideas, you will see much growth and equip them for fulfillment in school, career, and their own family life.

NOTES
1. Thomas Lickona, Ph.D., quoted in "Raising a Moral Child," *CHILD* Magazine, December/January 1993, page 130.
2. Rabbi Neil Kurshan quoted in *Imprimis*, vol. 20, no. 9, September 1992, page 3.
3. Charles Colson, "Know Your Terms," *Breakpoint*, 1993.
4. Senator Dan Coats, "America's Youth: A Crisis of Character," vol. 20, no. 9, September 1991, page 2.
5. Dr. Flip Flippen, family and adolescent counselor, Bryan, Texas, quoted from a personal interview.

1

Respect each family member's
right to privacy—bedroom, books,
other possessions.

2

Let your child
help you do volunteer work—
putting on mailing labels
for a charity fundraiser
or serving food
at a homeless shelter.

3

When your child leaves clothes, toys,
or other things lying around on the floor
of the living room,
gather them in a "Saturday Box"
where they are unattainable
until the next Saturday.
He will quickly learn to put things away
where they belong!

4

Give an award every evening at suppertime.
Get a red plate that says,
"You Are Special Today."
Put a list of admirable character qualities
on the refrigerator—
honesty, responsibility, enthusiasm, etc.
Through the day,
notice someone in the family
who deserves the "Red Plate Award"
because of a character quality she displays.
Then honor her by setting the plate
at her place at the table
and acknowledging out loud the particular
quality she's demonstrated.

5

To encourage the writing of thank-you's,
put pre-stamped blank thank-you cards
in your child's Christmas stocking.
Suggest that he write these notes
of appreciation on Christmas afternoon.

6

As much as possible,
as parents be a united front:
▶ verbally affirm your mate;
▶ avoid teaming up with your child
against your mate; ▶ support your mate's
disciplinary actions,
instead of changing the consequence
when the child complains.

7

Affirm with positive words
the kinds of behavior
you want from your child
and the kind of actions you expect:
"We use our indoor voices in the library."
"Words are for building people up,
not tearing them down."

8

Point out that our actions
have consequences.
Let your child know that if she chooses
to misbehave, for example,
she is choosing to experience a "timeout"
away from playmates
or other appropriate consequences.
Be certain to follow through.

9

An excellent way to teach your children
to work is to do chores *together*.
On Saturday morning,
divide responsibilities
for family household jobs
according to each person's abilities
and age. Give a choice of several jobs.
Write the jobs on paper,
hand out, and work for a specified amount
of time (one hour, for example).
Then go for ice cream or enjoy another
treat together.

10

Young people need heroes
as role models
they look up to and admire.
Find information about heroes—the
famous *and* the little-known,
from the past and the present—such as
David Livingstone, missionary
and scientist to Africa;
Dave Dravecky,
pro baseball pitcher
who lost his arm
and shoulder to cancer;
Joni Eareckson Tada, a quadriplegic
who is an outstanding author,
artist, and activist for handicapped
people's rights;
Dr. Fred Epstein, a neurosurgeon
who overcame learning disabilities
to become one
of the best in his field
and save the lives
of countless children.

11

Let your child accept responsibility
for the consequences when he deserves
them because of a wrongdoing,
instead of defending and rescuing.

—※—

12

Although you shop for a two-year-old's
clothes, you could let a preteen pick
her own outfits, give a fifteen-year-old
money to manage her own clothing
budget, and allow an eighteen-year-old
to manage a checking account
for clothing, gas, school expenses, etc.

—※—

13

Break down jobs
so they are manageable for your child.
Be patient—it takes a young child
longer to do a task than an adult.

14

"One day Matthew was helping me load
up tree limbs I had chain-sawed down.
I sliced up the limbs
of the big oak tree,
but they were too heavy for him to carry.
So I sliced them up again
with the chain saw,
but the pieces were still too heavy.
Finally, I sliced the wood even smaller,
and Matt could lift them.
He proudly carried load after load
to the truck. Not only did he learn
that dad was determined to work
with him; he saw me caring more
about him than about getting
the job done fast."
—FLIP FLIPPEN

———⟫∘⟪———

15

Don't just drop your kids off
at the church or synagogue.
If you want them to be involved,
participate in the activities yourself.

16

Encourage each child
to develop interests independent
of others based
on his or her bent,
and show appreciation
of each child's different pursuits.

———

17

Hold in confidence
the secrets your child tells you.

———

18

Encourage your children
to spend one-on-one time together
as siblings, without you,
so their bonds will grow stronger.

19

At dinner every night,
ask each family member to write
a small note with a blessing
he feels he received that day.
Place the notes in a "Thankful Basket,"
and once a week or on special occasions,
read the notes aloud
to remind everyone of the many good
things that happen each day.

20

Avoid paying your child
for high grades.
Your child may work for good grades
because they earn her monetary reward
rather than because she finds learning
useful or loves the activity.
The more children are paid to learn,
the harder it is for them to internalize
the value of learning
for its own sake.

21

"Children are constantly watching parents,
listening to what they say to each other
and checking to see
if words and deeds match."
—HENRY HOLSTEGE

———❖———

22

Material things
are never an adequate substitute
for parents spending time with their child
to take a walk, throw a baseball,
or discuss ideas.

———❖———

23

Be involved in school activities by finding
a way to contribute your skills
to enrich the learning experience of your
child and his classmates: Chaperon a field
trip, lead a reading group,
or tutor students who need extra help.

24

"Encourage small steps toward
your child's autonomy,
and gradually transfer responsibility
so that when your child is beyond
your control,
he or she will no longer need it."
—Dr. James Dobson

25

Set realistic limits
concerning curfews,
household chores,
and other family guidelines.

26

Don't protect your child
from the consequences of her mistakes.
When you rescue her,
she learns dependence
and irresponsibility.

27

Keep small note pads
and pens by each phone in your home.
Teach your child to answer the phone
politely and write down the message
for the family member who was called.
Have a central place
to leave messages.

28

When your child breaks curfew
or makes a mistake: ▶ Don't vent your
pent-up frustrations.
▶ Impose penalties appropriate
for the mistake. ▶ Stand by him
and be available.
▶ Help with problem solving,
but make the child
own the problem.
▶ Share information needed
to deal with the mistake.

29

It's a great danger to buy the behavior
we want from our kids.
Research shows that many American
parents give things as a way of avoiding
confrontations with their children.

—◆—

30

Find a balance between rigidity
and permissiveness in your parenting.
Positive, authoritative parents—who
enforce standards, talk things over, engage
in joint decision making,
and show lots of warmth—raise more
responsible, higher achieving teens.

—◆—

31

Be there for your child when you are
needed, stay out of the way when she can
do something on her own, and be wise
enough to recognize the difference.

32

Hard work deserves a reward.
Every time you and your child
work hard and finish
a big job or project, celebrate!
Get a double malt or a pizza,
and applaud a job well done.

33

Admit it when you have made a mistake.

34

If there is a problem, don't judge your
child without listening to his explanation
as he accounts for his behavior.

35

Express your beliefs.

36

Define and reflect your child's feelings.
For example, you could say,
"You seem to be feeling sad today.
What's happening at school?"

—◆—

37

Help your child
learn to be resourceful
in play by giving her a great big box
to make into a playhouse,
fort, or castle
(or several smaller ones
that can be duct-taped together
into a tunnel).

—◆—

38

Ask questions that require
more than a yes or no answer to open up
communication with your child.

39

Invite your child
to share his opinions with you on a variety
of subjects—on controversial issues
at school and in the community,
on national issues.

40

With a plain, unlined spiral notebook,
let your child write in her favorite recipes,
use ink stamps to decorate the pages,
bright markers and paints
to illustrate the finished products,
and present it to a grandparent or teacher.

41

Incorporating "why" or "why not"
questions into your conversations
helps your child become a better
conversationalist and thinker.

42

Laugh at your child's jokes,
riddles, and humorous stories.

———◆◆———

43

With your child in tow,
and a hammer for each of you,
join together in a Habitat for Humanity
house-building project
in your community.

———◆◆———

44

"If children are given encouragement
to think about moral issues
and to use their capacity
to examine those issues reflectively,
then I think their moral life grows
and becomes stronger."
—ROBERT COLES

45

No matter how much
your teen "pulls on the rope"
or pushes on the boundaries,
don't let go of your end—keep providing
support and structure,
and increase responsibilities
and privileges as he grows.

46

Once a week
bring a clipping
of a newspaper article
or current magazine to talk about
at the dinner table,
and discuss the event or issue,
its possible impact,
and what each person's
opinion is of it.

47

As a family, sponsor a child in a Third-World country through a reputable organization like Feed the Children, World Vision, Compassion International, etc. Write to the child, keep his or her picture on your bulletin board or refrigerator, and save money in a central place for each person's regular contribution to the child's support.

48

Instead of a typical vacation, take a mercy trip together as a family to a part of North America that needs help—even a local inner city area.

49

Always treat your mate politely—say please and thank you to him or her. Your child is watching!

50

Have a "Family History Day."
Get out records
of your family history:
genealogical charts,
letters, photos, deeds,
marriage certificates,
birth records.
Show these things
to your child, and talk about talents
and aptitudes that parents
and grandparents
have passed down
to different children
in your family as "gifts."

51

Show appreciation
for your child's teacher
by sending a note of thanks
for special reading contests, field trips,
and extra help he or she gives your child.

52

It's important to merit
your child's respect.
Children who show respect
for their parents pay more attention
in school and more attention
to coaches and other adults.

53

Let your child accept full responsibility
for her homework,
instead of picking up the burden
and doing it for her if she falls down
on the job.

54

Teachers can most effectively reinforce
qualities like honesty, respect,
and responsibility when they are building
upon foundations already
established by parents.

55

Limit your child's television intake
as much as possible.
Preschoolers and pre-readers should
watch no more than five hours of carefully
selected programming per week,
and older children should not watch
much more than that.
Instead, encourage them to play,
do sports, read, help around the house,
talk with parents and others.

56

Convince your child that education
is important and that you expect him
to do the best he possibly can in school.

57

Have your child practice using
the telephone and being courteous while
asking for information (e.g., to compare
prices or check on movie times).

58

Provide materials—brushes,
paints, charcoal, colored pencils,
and different kinds of paper—
for permanent pictures your child
can create and give to friends
and relatives as gifts.
Keep old frames and buy
inexpensive ones to frame the art.

59

Studies show that Asian-American
students often excel in school
because their family values
of respect for education, hard work,
and parental support to achieve
are much higher than in the traditional
American family—not because
they are smarter than
other children.

60

Ask the teacher for help
in challenging your child:
If she has mastered the grade-level math,
ask that she be given some work
on a higher level
or an independent study
in an area of her interest.

61

Create an environment
of teamwork in your home
by working together
on an outdoor project:
raking and disposing
of the mounds of fall leaves
or washing and waxing
the cars.

62

Help your child see that we often have
the most growth in our characters
through trials and struggles,
and teach him to embrace them
instead of run from them.
Share examples of your own difficulties
and how you grew through them
or stories of people
in your community who have
overcome a problem.

63

Talk with your child about the future
and what it holds. Help her look ahead
to know what she can be doing
now to prepare for the future.
Get a book on different careers,
visit the workplace of someone
in a vocation that interests her,
then figure out what courses are needed
in high school and college
for the job she hopes for.

64

Emphasize to your child
that what is important to achieve
is not just good grades but
also "stick-to-itiveness":
coming back from a failure on a test,
sports competition,
or relationship.

65

Teach your child to
"Let every knock be a boost,"
or how to learn from hardship.
If he runs for student council and loses,
suggest he stay involved,
watch his student leaders,
and try again.
If he doesn't do well
on a test after studying,
suggest he ask the teacher how he
can study differently next time.

66

Help your child find a way
to serve in your neighborhood
through a project, such as cutting
or watering the grass for an elderly person
or tutoring another child
with learning problems.
It will help her develop a pattern
of focusing on others
instead of just herself.

67

Show your child the value
of living things by watching
barn swallows or other birds
that come back every year,
build nests, and lay eggs.
Put up a bird feeder and clay tray
with water.

68

Encourage your child to give 110 percent
effort in whatever he does, whether
at home, school, or on the playing field.

69

Let your child help you tackle new tasks,
whether it's changing a tire
or cleaning out the garage,
so she will feel that she is a needed
and worthwhile part of the family.

70

"My mom never used the words
failure or 'You won't measure up' with me.
Whether it was a physics class
I had a hard time with or losing a spot
on the basketball team,
she always encouraged me,
and said, 'Keep trying.'"
—TINA PERRY

71

When a crisis hits and you lose
your temper, blow it,
or just don't handle it well,
let your child see you take two
steps back and say, "I blew it,
but I will do better next time."

72

Paint pictures in your child's mind
of strong character by telling stories
of men and women like
Paul Revere and Florence Nightingale
and great religious heroes
like Moses and David.

73

Be a model of someone who puts
his or her own talents to work
and share your achievements
with your children.

74

Encourage your child's efforts
by showing him how pleased
you are when he tries hard and finishes:
"You worked so hard!
It's wonderful how much
effort you put out
for that science project."

75

Help each of your
children make and decorate a chart
for tracking their success
on the character quality they
are working on or the goal
they hope to accomplish.
Tack the charts on a special
bulletin board.

76

Have a family motto for each month,
with the application visually depicted.
Post it on the refrigerator
or bulletin board,
so everyone can learn it. Try these:
- ► Forgive and forget.
- ► Honor one another.
- ► When at first you don't succeed,
  try, try again!
- ► Treat others like you want them
  to treat you.

77

Keep a dictionary handy,
and when there are questions
about definitions of words that come up
in daily conversation or reading,
someone can look
them up quickly.

78

Make a banner for your child's room
with bright felt letters, with the saying,
"No one can make you feel inferior
without your permission."
Discuss how this applies to everyday life
at school, sports, and with friends.

79

When your child asks you for permission
to do something—participate in a party,
activity, or spend money—instead of saying
no, ask her to "Make a Proposal," consisting
of who, what, why, when, and where in
writing. Then consider the proposal.

80

"Words are not unimportant,
but when parents say, in effect,
'Do as I say, not as I do,' it's reasonable
to predict that kids will do just the opposite."
—HENRY HOLSTEGE

81

Tell stories about when you were a child, including mistakes you made and what you learned from them.

———◆◆———

82

Help your child develop logical, deductive reasoning skills by playing thinking games such as Battleship and Mastermind.

———◆◆———

83

Join a tree-planting project in your neighborhood or town on Arbor Day, or organize a planting day yourself.

———◆◆———

84

Debate current issues, especially those that lend themselves to pro-and-con argument, and help young people form their own opinions.

85

Help your child develop
problem-solving strategies.
When he gets a telescope
for Christmas, although it's quicker to say,
"Let me show you how to do this,"
instead say, "I wonder what
would happen if you do this?"
Children who can problem-solve
and figure things out
are more motivated to seek out
information and not
as afraid of failure.

86

Never compare your child's work
or grades with another child's
or sibling's achievements.
Comparisons increase fears about
not measuring up.
Instead, appreciate your child's
unique qualities.

87

Give your child
an opportunity for input
into family decisions:
where to go on family night,
what extracurricular activities
to pursue, or who to invite over
for Sunday supper.

88

Develop a respect
for animals and responsibility
by having your child be responsible
(with demonstration and supervision
at first) for feeding, watering,
and exercising a family pet
on a daily basis.

89

Give your child a small plot
of ground to plant a vegetable
or flower garden. She can plant, water,
weed, and harvest the garden.
Besides learning responsibility,
she'll learn quickly the principle
of sowing and reaping: If she weeds and
waters, the plants grow;
if she doesn't, they die.

90

Help your child set goals in school
and work toward them.
Make a poster
with a ladder leading
to the desired goal
(bring C up to B in history)
and the three or four steps he can take
to "climb" and achieve it
(read ahead, study orally with a partner,
make and take a practice test).

91

Get families together
who share your values of effort
and achievement and who
emphasize school work.
If children have friends
who work hard and take
pride in their work,
they are more likely to put forth
effort and succeed.

92

Fill your child's life
with people of excellence—
teachers, religious and community
leaders, and other parents.
Invite them to dinner,
dialogue with them,
and discover the qualities
in their lives that led
to excellence.

93

Keep alert to what fuels your child's
motivation. At age five it may be Batman,
whales, and snakes. But at age ten, she
may be interested in building
and launching model rockets and doing
chemistry experiments. Kids' interests
often show up in their conversation
and questions. Go with her interests,
even if they are not your "cup of tea."

94

When things get hard, help your child
learn perseverance by saying,
"Press on—you're going to make it."
"We're proud of you for hanging in there
with your soccer team even though you
haven't won any games yet," or
"That's a really long assignment, but stick
with it and you'll get the problems done."
If the job seems overwhelming, divide it
into two or three blocks and encourage
a break in between.

95

Learning the importance
of organizational skills begins
in kindergarten.
Give your child a backpack
with a pouch for notes
from teacher and a pouch
for completed homework.
Designate a certain place by the door
for him to put it when he
comes home from school along
with books, Show and Tell objects,
and anything else needed
for the next day.

96

If your young child wants to help
with a difficult job at home,
teach her how to do it—
go through each step, let her try,
and you'll be boosting her sense
of initiative. Even if the results
aren't as perfect as if you'd done it,
say something positive about her efforts.

97

Provide a "Family Activity Center"
on a table in a corner of the kitchen,
family room, or other space
with the raw materials
of creation—paper, crayons,
glue, scissors, glitter, stickers, etc.

———◈———

98

To avoid squashing your child's
budding sense of initiative,
resist remaking his bed or rewriting
the stories or poems he's written so they
will sound better or get a higher grade.

———◈———

99

"Kind words can be short and easy
to speak, but their echoes
are truly endless."
—MOTHER TERESA

100

Give your child an inexpensive camera
and encourage her to take photos of items
of interest at home,
in the neighborhood,
and on trips and outings.

101

If your child likes mechanical things,
take him to a junkyard to get things
to take apart and put together
in a different way. Add boards, nails,
and a few tools, and he can invent some
creative objects and machines.

102

While eating dinner together as a family,
go around the table and take turns
answering the questions: "What was
the high point in your day?"
and "What was the low point?"

103

Make a creativity kit for your child,
giving her opportunities
to be resourceful and inventive.
Gather bright, interesting materials
that are versatile and allow
for individual creativity:
neon pom-poms, pipe cleaners,
Styrofoam trays, squares of fabric,
cardboard mailing tubes, paper rolls,
markers, glitter, felt squares, etc.

104

Beginning in kindergarten,
have your child give a Valentine's card
to every student in the class,
even if the teacher doesn't require it.
Sometimes children give cards only
to their friends, but it will be worth
the extra cards if even one
child gets a Valentine who otherwise
might not have.

105

Your child is likely to live up to what
you believe of him.
Have high expectations.

106

The best way to teach character is to have
it around the home.

107

Be a "homework consultant" with your
child by offering to go over a math problem
or orally drill for spelling or a foreign
language if she needs your help.

108

"Live so that you wouldn't be ashamed to
sell the family parrot to the town gossip."
—WILL ROGERS

109

Give a child a fish and he can eat
for a day. Teach a child to fish
and he can eat for a lifetime.

—————◆—————

110

Play the game "Inventor"
in the car to stimulate thinking
and coming up with solutions,
a vital skill in problem-solving.
Ask questions: What are all the uses
you can think of for an old tire,
an empty ice-cream cone,
a shoe box? How many different things
can you do with a ball
or with hamburger meat?

—————◆—————

111

A good example has twice the value
of good advice.

112

"The most important work you will do . . .
will be within the walls
of your own home."
—HAROLD B. LEE

———◆———

113

Teach your child that the secret
of contentment is to enjoy what she has.
Here's an exercise to cultivate
contentment: Think about how
happy you would be if you
lost everything you have right now
and then got it back again.

———◆———

114

"If you want your children
to turn out well, spend twice as
much time with them,
and half as much money."
—ABIGAIL VAN BUREN

115

If you have a home
business, give your child
age-appropriate tasks
that contribute—folding letters,
stamping checks for deposit
(young child); filing,
typing, filling mail orders,
photocopying
(older kids).

116

Talk to your child
about peer pressure,
guiding him about when
family values and personal
convictions or inclinations
should outweigh
the influence of friends.

117

"The tragedy of our times
is that our young people are being
taught that they must never make
a mistake—that to make
a mistake is unforgivable.
All great men have made mistakes.
If you're afraid of making a mistake,
then it means you will stop functioning."
—ELEANOR ROOSEVELT

118

Set aside twenty to thirty minutes each
day for reading aloud—just a time for you
and your child.

119

Ask your child what she thinks about
issues rather than telling her
what to think.

120

Be consistent about the values
you are acting out:
If you have stressed
the importance of honesty to your child,
tell your friends the truth
when you can't go to dinner
with them.

121

Many children don't try new things
because they fear failure.
Share that failing at a few things
doesn't make a person a failure
and no one can win all the time.
Then read about people who failed
but made outstanding
contributions—Jonas Salk,
Thomas Edison, Winston Churchill,
Pearl Buck.

122

Set aside a time for problem-solving
as a family. Give each person a blank index
card and have him write down
a household problem he sees. Shuffle the
cards and read them one by one.
Brainstorm and have a recorder write
down all the possible solutions
and what their outcomes might be.
Arrive at a consensus of the best plan
of action, write it on the card, and go on
to the next problem.

123

Help your child deal with failure by asking:
► Why did I fail?—looking
at what she did wrong
(rather than blaming someone else).
► How can I improve,
or what can I learn
for next time?

124

Cut out an article on a current
political action, new tax, or legislation.
Outline the main points of the issue
and the proposed action and then discuss:
How can we look at this a different way?
Does it really have to be this way?
In what other ways could the people
responsible deal with the problem?
Who could we contact?

125

It is important that children
learn where to get help.
Draw the outline of your child's
hand, and have him cut it out.
Then on each finger write a way
to get help, such as: ask parents
and siblings; look it up; watch someone
else; take lessons; ask a friend.
Put the hand on the bulletin board
or refrigerator and talk about when each
option could best be used.

126

Help your child learn to follow
directions by: ▶ breaking a task
into small bites; ▶ writing down
directions and crossing them off.
Start with a few directions
and build to longer,
more complex ones.
Encourage her along the way.

———◆———

127

Once a month celebrate
the birthday of someone who has
made a big contribution to society
and who has character traits
to admire—a scientist,
composer, author.
Get a book or article about
the person to read, play their music,
or learn information about them.
Talk about their character, convictions,
and actions.

128

As a family, design and make a flag
that expresses your strengths,
heritage, values, and hobbies.
Divide a rectangular piece of bright
felt into four sections.
Each section will have a symbol
or symbols that reflect the above four
areas (*examples:* sense of humor;
ancestors' national heritage; love of family
and country; camping, hiking,
and reading). The flag can be attached
to a wooden dowel and displayed
on family occasions and holidays.

129

Read your child a wise saying
from the book of Proverbs
in the Bible each morning.
Discuss how it applies to everyday life.
You could have your child draw
an illustration of it or write a story
that demonstrates it.

130

When you have trouble with something,
point it out to your child. While fixing
a water hose outside or cleaning
and reorganizing a closet, you could say,
"See, I'm a bit frustrated and would
like to get this finished, but I'm going
to keep figuring and working and find
a way to solve it."

———◆———

131

At the grocery store,
give your child practice
in following directions.
Say: "Please get me the box of tea
that's caffeine free and on sale this week.
See, it's on the bottom shelf.
Great, now let's look on aisle 4 for
the juices—can you get me one can
of frozen apple juice, three of orange
juice, and two lemonades?"
Continue throughout
your shopping.

132

When your child starts collecting
things, help him organize them
instead of letting them
clutter up his room.
Collectibles can be stored
in shoe boxes, egg cartons,
clear plastic bins,
albums and notebooks,
on shelves.

133

Instead of buying a new
store-bought toy, stir up your child's
resourcefulness by giving her
several parts of some
favorite games or toys
(or odds and ends
of invention from around your home)
and suggesting she combine
them to make a new
game or toy.

134

Sing a familiar song and suggest your child
make up a brand-new verse or chorus.

135

When you visit grandparents
or great-grandparents, ask them to find
special memorabilia or treasures and while
showing them to your child, tell
the stories behind them or the significance
of them: a clock, wedding ring,
photograph, medal, or trophy.

136

Be aware of the values in the stories
and books you read to your child.
Think about: Does the author portray
the characters in the story with qualities
you hope to develop in your child's life?
What values does the "hero" live by?
After reading, talk about the story
and the character qualities.

137

To encourage thoughtfulness,
make breakfast
in bed when a family
member has a birthday
or is convalescing,
and ask your child to help
prepare the food
and deliver it.

———◆———

138

To encourage consideration,
when a parent or sibling
is taking a nap, say to your child,
"Dad is taking a nap now;
let's quietly tiptoe so we don't
wake him up."

139

To encourage perseverance,
when you see your child frustrated
at learning something,
whether it is sports or homework,
explain how much pianists and gymnasts
(or your child's favorite musician
or athlete) have to practice before suc-
ceeding in a big competition.
To be really good at something, we must
practice a skill over and over and keep
working even when frustrated.

140

To encourage your child to treat others
the way he'd like to be treated,
role play. Say, "Let's pretend you
prepared a special dinner and invited a
friend over to eat, and he said,
'I don't like this. What else do you have?'
How would you feel?
Would you want to have him
over again for dinner?"

141

Provide a children's Bible
for your child, one with illustrations
and easy-to-understand language.
Read about the characters, struggles,
stories, and wisdom,
and relate them
to everyday life.

———◆———

142

"In the daily course of events,
describe to your child
what she has accomplished
so that little by little she can get a picture
of herself as capable and responsible
(or punctual, or whatever
good quality you see).
'You said you'd be back at 7:00,
and you're right on time.
That's what I call punctuality!'"
—ADELE FABER

143

Invite a foreign-exchange student
to share a meal with your family.
Offering hospitality to a student
who may be 10,000 miles away
from his or her family
is a wonderful example of caring
for others, and your child can learn
to appreciate another culture
at the same time.

144

"Use a 'Yes, Ma'am' Can to encourage
good manners and a positive response
from young children
when you ask them to do something
for you. If they reply
with a 'Yes, Ma'am' (minus any argument
or complaining) they can pull out a coin
from a can filled with pennies,
nickels, and dimes."
—RUTHANN WINANS

145

Share with your child a time when prayer
or meditation made a difference
in your life, changed a situation,
or changed your attitude about it.

146

Together with your child
write a letter to the editor
of your local paper.
Using a current issue you have
discussed and formed an opinion about,
help him outline the letter,
highlighting the points and backing
them up with facts.

147

To encourage your child to talk
in a cheerful, hopeful way, help her make
a list of all the positive things she said
today. Suggest she increase the positive
words tomorrow.

148

Referring to a role model
in a favorite story can help young
children gain the momentum to keep
trying on a difficult task.
For example, "Remember the Little
Engine That Could;
although he had never been over
the mountain and it looked like
an impossible task to pull all
the toys and dolls,
as he pulled and tugged and said
'I think I can . . . I think I can,' slowly at
first, he did!"

149

Instead of placing emphasis
on innate ability or IQ,
focus on the progress your child
can make with hard work and effort—
whether at school or home.

150

Make time to do things
with your spouse or your own friends.
Children learn from
observation how important
relationships are.

———◆———

151

"Problem solvers look
at seemingly overwhelming
situations and come up with ideas
for making them better.
Problem solvers view all situations,
even terrible tragedies,
as positive learning experiences.
Problem solvers do not feel
helpless or flounder.
They are not vulnerable
to other people's control."
—ANTOINETTE SAUNDERS

152

Fan the flame of your child's curiosity
by keeping a sense of wonder
and discovery about the world around
you: If it rains, take your umbrella
and splash through puddles together.
If it thunders, take shelter and count
to determine how far away the storm is.
(Count the seconds from the moment you
see lightning until you hear thunder
and divide by five to measure
how many miles you are from the center
of the storm.)

153

Expose your child to a wide variety
of things in the world and see what really
grabs her interest. Once she shows
genuine, serious interest, then help her
pursue it by providing resources,
lessons or practice,
and role models.

154

Teach your child never to be afraid
of asking questions, especially *"Why?"*
because that's how we learn.

155

Provide a big trunk or box
of dress-up clothes, hats, shoes, etc.,
so that your child and friends or siblings
can create characters, role-play,
tell stories, and have fun.

156

Instill the value of hospitality in your child
by having someone to your home at least
one meal a week. Rotate a different family
member inviting a guest each week.
Include your child in the menu planning,
preparation, making an interesting
centerpiece, and giving guests a warm
welcome as they arrive.

157

During chore times and on a daily basis,
use statements that encourage effort like:
- ► Keep up the good work!
- ► You catch on so fast—
you're doing a terrific job.
- ► You are working so efficiently
and making great use
of your time!
- ► I'm so proud of the way you've
worked today.

158

When your child brings home papers
from school, ask him to evaluate them so
he can begin to assess his own work.
(Does he like it and feel it's his best work,
or does he think it's a mess? On a report
card, is he pleased with each subject's
grade, or would he like to bring one up?)
Then ask what ways he'd like to improve
it, and what steps it would take
to accomplish that.

159

Take your child
to used bookstores and bookfairs
and help her build her own personal
"library on a shoestring" of favorite
biographies, novels, books of poetry,
and classics.

160

Encourage an enthusiastic outlook toward
things your child does by saying, "This will
be fun and exciting; we'll learn something
new through this," even if the task
or experience looks boring,
childish, or difficult.

161

Show your child how to keep track of all
income received and spent by creating his
own "Budget Book." Have divisions
on the page for Credits (Money In), Debits
(Money Spent), and other categories.

162

When your child dives into homework assignments on her own initiative, praise her and let her know how valuable it is to do things without being reminded.

163

Encourage your child to be merciful to those who are hurting or needy by brainstorming on a service project each year that you can do as a family. Let him be involved in researching community needs and deciding what action to take.

164

To help your child learn to be comfortable in front of a group, give her opportunities to sing with a group in school or church or to teach the rest of the family something she knows how to do.

165

"Share a vision of your child
or teen making
a contribution to society:
'I love that point you made about
the homeless problem;
you seem to really care about that.
You're the kind of person who
could turn that around.'
Or say, 'There are going to be
a lot of people who need
your convictions.'"
—ADELE FABER

166

Discuss moral situations
at the dinner table:
why we don't park in handicapped zones,
whether to give money
to panhandlers,
why drugs are destructive.

167

Use a variety of positive statements
that stimulate initiative:
► You are really motivated!
► I like the way you've tackled
that job without being asked!
► You've been a self-starter,
setting the alarm early
and doing your piano practice
before school.

———◆———

168

When your child goofs,
instead of telling him what
his mistake was, ask questions like,
"How would you do this next time?"
or "What did you learn
from this situation?"
This will help him think
through and plan
for next time.

169

Instill a grateful attitude in your child
by overseeing private verbal
"thank you's" to others who have helped
her or been kind.

170

Encourage an appreciation for history
by occasionally doing things the
"old-fashioned way": Make butter
from whipping cream, handwash clothes
and hang out to dry, go to an antique shop
or living history museum.

171

Cultivate a love for the outdoors
by camping with your child. Cook over
a fire, take a hike, follow animal tracks,
sleep in a tent, gaze at the stars
in the night sky, and enjoy
the great outdoors!

172

Make a game out of remembering
to put your napkins in your lap
before eating: If someone doesn't
have a napkin in his or her lap
before the first bite,
that person has to run up and down
the stairs one time singing
"Mary Had a Little Lamb"—this includes
parents, children, and even guests!

173

Take your child to a local
retirement center once a month
to visit with residents who
don't have other visitors.
He could sing or play an instrument
for them, play a board game
with them, or just hug them.
Together you could send a card
to some of these special
seniors on birthdays
and holidays.

174

Cultivate an appreciation
of nature and care of living things
by raising tadpoles, caterpillars,
a duckling, or another small animal,
and then taking it to the best
habitat nearby to live
when it's ready to flee
from your "nest."

175

To build organizational values,
help your child begin a coin collection
and store in small zip-lock or felt bags.
Save older coins going
out of circulation, one new coin
from each category:
penny, nickel, dime, etc.
When friends visit another country,
ask them to bring back coins.

176

Stimulate your child's powers
of observation by encouraging her
to make full use of her eyes and ears
in the world of nature:
to observe the rapid fluttering
of the hummingbird at the feeder,
the delicate web of the spider at dawn.
Provide a magnifying glass
for a closer look.

177

Give your child a spiral "camp notebook"
for keeping a record of summer camp
experiences and friends. On several pages
write a different question for him
to answer each day, like "Describe your
bunkmate and something you did
together." Besides having a record
of camp each year, a place for new friends'
phone numbers and addresses,
and a place for photographs, he can talk
about some of those experiences
when he gets home.

178

Take your child to "Toastmasters" meetings so she can develop public speaking skills while you develop your own communication skills.

179

To help your child do a task thoroughly and responsibly: ▶ Walk him through the job several times—e.g., how to clean/mop the floor; ▶ spot-check and show him how to re-do if needed; ▶ explain to him how necessary a clean floor is to your family and how important his help is; ▶ comment on how clean and shiny the floor looks when he's done.

180

To appreciate nature:
Go to a nearby park or forest, plot a small area of ground with markers and string, and return every six weeks or so and draw how things have changed.

181

During your child's stressful times,
let up on your demands.

182

In the summer months, enlist your child
to help you serve "Meals on Wheels"
to the elderly and handicapped
in your community.

183

Whatever your child's "passion"
or burning interest, provide a large album
and suggest she make a scrapbook.
A child fascinated by jets and airplanes
could make an aeronautical scrapbook;
another, an animal scrapbook;
another, one on foreign countries
she'd like to visit with pictures
and postcards from travel agencies.

184

"Firm direction with the proper voice
control is powerful,
convincing, and encouraging."
—ZIG ZIGLAR

185

At family birthday dinners,
have each person
share something he admires
about the person
on his right.

186

Offer to help your mate
with her chores
and let her help you with yours.
Kids see this cooperation
and follow your lead.

187

Have one more wrapped package
for your child to open only upon
the completion of thank-you notes
for birthday gifts and other occasions
when appreciation needs to be expressed.

188

If you have a problem with your children
forgetting to take lunches, assignments,
etc., to school, give them one "free"
delivery per year. After that,
each trip costs them a certain amount
of "taxi fare" to Mom or Dad
(depending on the distance between
home and school).

189

By eight or nine years old,
boys can be taught to open restaurant
doors and mall doors for their mother
or other girls.

190

Teach your child how to meet adults:
Instead of standing back and waiting for
them to say hello, walk up to a person,
stick out your hand, and say, "Hi, my name
is . . . ," and look them straight in the eye.

191

Encourage your child
to call her out-of-town grandparents
at least once a month to see how they
are doing and to share news.

192

To teach your child to appreciate his
belongings, have a guideline: Keep it nice
and take care of it, or lose it temporarily.
(If it's left out in the rain,
instead of being put away in the child's
room, he loses its use for a week.)

193

On your child's birthday,
ask how she wants to grow:
personally, relationally, and spiritually.

194

If you will be late to an appointment or
friend's home because your child
isn't organized or has dawdled,
have him call and let the person know
that you are running late.

195

"The day each child was born I promised
to teach him or her *one thing* each day,
not necessarily big things, but a gift for
each day: put her napkin in her lap,
to say 'thank you,' how to set the table
graciously for dinner."
—JESSIE ANN ARNOLD
What one thing can you teach
your child today?

196

"A man's success
is made up of failures,
because he experiments and ventures
every day. . . . I have heard
that in horsemanship he is not
the good rider who never was thrown,
but rather that a man will never be
a good rider until he is thrown;
then he will not be haunted any longer
by the terror that he shall tumble,
and will ride whither he is bound."
—RALPH WALDO EMERSON

197

Make a pleasant work place
for homework. If the "study zone"
is on the kitchen table, for instance,
provide sharpened pencils,
erasers, paper, a glass of juice,
and even flowers.

198

Designate three different envelopes
for your child to manage her allowance
and additional money:
one for 10 percent toward church
or charity; one for saving 40 percent;
one for the remaining 50 percent
to be spent on her choice
of activities.

———◆———

199

When your child has a friend over,
suggest he bring out only toys or food
that he is willing to share.

———◆———

200

Help your child cultivate
a pen-pal relationship
with a cousin or family member
in another state
by writing regular letters.

201

Talk with your child about what she is learning at school.

202

Provide plenty of emotional support to your child throughout his growing up and adolescent years by patient listening, unconditional love, and affection.

203

Talking to a small child at her eye level gives us a different perspective on the world and lets her know we are really listening and interested in what she has to say.

204

When you wash your young child's clothes, teach him how to sort the dirty ones before washing, then to fold them and put them away in proper places.

205

Let your child help you with a new task
and figure out together how to do it—
changing the tire on your car,
checking the oil, etc.

206

Don't overload your child with too much
equipment when she shows an interest
in something. If she starts collecting rocks,
don't rush out and buy an expensive kit.
Give her a minimum amount of materials
at first, and as her response
is positive and she takes care of those
materials, supply more.

207

If your child is not taking care of
the materials you provide for drawing,
music, sports, a collection,
or other interest, even after you've shown
him how to take care of them,
then remove the materials.

208

Give your child time to daydream,
do nothing, or make her own fun.
When we overschedule
her day with planned activities
or overstuff her with facts
and abstract knowledge,
a child has no time to pursue her own
interests or develop resourcefulness.

209

"Teaching etiquette
is the kindest thing you can do
for your child.
It predates law and everything else
in getting along with other people.
You can't get away
without etiquette any more
than you can decide
not to use language."
—JUDITH MARTIN

210

Take time to do creative things
along with your child:
Sketch a tree in the country,
make a homemade kite to fly
or a paper boat to sail.

211

When faced with a decision,
help your child weigh options
by making a pro-and-con list.
Have him draw a line
down the middle of a piece of paper.
On the right side he can write
"Pro" and list all the reasons
to do something—i.e., to buy an item:
the benefits, how he'll use and enjoy it.
On the left side,
he can write "Con"
and all the reasons *not* to spend money
on that item
(or whatever the situation).

212

Michael Josephson suggests a litmus test
for parents' actions: How would you act if
you knew your child were looking over
your shoulder?

213

Talk about the character traits you admire
the most. Share with your child
why the qualities are important to you
and how as a family you can strive to build
them into your lives.

214

Let your child help solve practical
problems around your home and yard:
figure out how far apart to space shrubs
in a row, fix the mixer, or plan a family trip.
When kids work with *real* problems,
they become confident in their
problem-solving ability.

215

Talk intelligently to your preschooler,
naming things aloud,
talking about what's going on
in the world around her,
and answering her questions
with interest.

216

Encourage your child to write,
for writing pushes children
to organize their thoughts
more than any other activity.

217

Play energetic marching music
in the morning
to begin the day
and soothing classical music
in the evening before bed.

218

"Let your child know:
'I love you enough
to insist on a curfew,
to discipline you if you have liquor
on your breath,
to chaperon your parties,
to take the time to be
at your athletic contests,
your musical presentations,
your academic events.'"
—HENRY HOLSTEGE

219

When your child
has a novel to read for school,
"share" the reading by getting the book
yourself in paperback
or at the library
and reading it independently.
This can open up great dialogue
between you.

220

When your child has a big assignment
or project looming in front of him,
encourage him to: ▶ write down a list
of what he has to do; ▶ assign each item
a priority order; ▶ list the steps by which
he can accomplish the tasks.

———◆———

221

Enroll your child in a Junior Great Books
group in the summer or after school
in which each member of the group reads
the classics and then they meet
to discuss challenging questions
on interpretation and other issues.

———◆———

222

Provide a small notebook for your child
or teenager to write down her daily "To
Do" and "To Call" lists to keep her focused
and prevent her from feeling
overwhelmed by the demands of school
and home responsibilities.

223

Using poster board,
markers, glitter,
and sequins (jewels), make crowns.
Whenever a family member
shows a willingness
to put others' needs ahead of his own,
pitch in, or serve others,
crown him "King" (or "Queen")
at supper, demonstrating
the principle that leaders
must learn to serve
and help others.

224

Don't permit putdown humor
in your home,
when children consistently tease
one another,
make fun of a younger sibling,
or use biting sarcasm.

225

Let your child
assist with a garage sale:
lettering signs, distributing flyers
on her bike in the neighborhood,
pricing items,
and acting as a "salesperson"
on garage sale day.
After a few years
of experience,
she can coordinate
a single-family
or block yard sale.

226

When your older child
begins receiving
a monthly clothing allowance,
attach the responsibility to do his own
laundry, including ironing,
and take care
of the clothes purchased.

227

Help your child look
for something positive
in each person
regardless of his or her race
or socioeconomic level
by pointing out a strength
or admirable
character quality you see.
Show there is much to be learned
about people from different cultures
and backgrounds.

228

Follow through
and do what you say
you are going to do with your child,
even (and especially)
if it is inconvenient.
In the process,
you will be modeling
the keeping of one's word.

229

Have your child
call her out-of-town grandparents
whenever she has done
something special.
If she begins these occasional
across-the-miles-chats when she is young
and continues through the teenage years,
their relationship will grow.

———◆———

230

"One day when I was in the third grade
both of my parents took me
to the bank to open a savings account.
It was in my name,
and I received a savings passbook.
My parents told me
that I could put in any amount I wanted,
but I always had to save something
if I received money.
I have had a growing savings account
ever since!"
—TRAVIS VAUGHN (college senior)

231

Respect the differences
of opinion each family member has,
no matter his or her age,
by "agreeing to disagree"
when discussing a controversial matter
or an issue with different sides to it.

232

Seek help in your community or church
when you need it. Show your child how
to ask for help by role-playing
(you be the teacher and have your child
ask for extra help on homework,
then let your child act as the principal
and you ask for help).

233

Major on the majors—
pick a few issues and boundaries
that are important to you with regard
to household rules and *stick to them*.

234

Confront problems head-on.
Denying problems
or avoiding trouble spots builds stress
in the family
and teaches irresponsibility.

235

Find a variety of little ways to incorporate
your religious beliefs
and faith into everyday life.

236

Provide materials and ideas for your child
to *make* gifts for grandparents and special
relatives for Christmas and birthdays
instead of buying presents with
your money: a T-shirt with his hand prints
in bright colors, a framed piece
of art he created, fragrant potpourri,
or other gifts
will be treasured for years.

237

Avoid taking your child out of school
for vacations, shopping excursions,
and other non-medical reasons.
Doing so may send
a message that school is not important.

238

Don't direct "putdowns" at your spouse.
When parents voice respect for each
other, kids tend to respect their parents
and each other.

239

"When my siblings and I were doing
unpleasant jobs around the house,
our mother encouraged us to pretend like
we were old fashioned
English housemaids.
It made working hard lots of fun."
—ANDREA MARSHALL (college student)

240

After giving general guidelines,
allow your child
to lay out clothes the night before
and dress herself independently
each morning. Kids who dress themselves
on their own, without being nagged,
arrive in the classroom
feeling more confident.

241

Verbalize your expectations
positively:
"I hope you can get
your spelling test studied for
so we can play Monopoly after dinner.
That would be fun for the whole family,"
instead of using
negative statements or threats
("If you don't get
your math homework done,
you can't play Monopoly with us").

242

Show your child
how to put important,
frequently used things in the same place
every day until it becomes automatic.
Demonstrate how putting your keys
(or another item) on the same hook each
evening keeps you from wasting time
looking for them.
Then find appropriate places for his
school and personal belongings
and insist he put them there daily for six
weeks, until the habit has formed.

243

Use logical consequences:
If your children are to turn out their
bedroom lights but they consistently leave
them on, unscrew the light bulbs.
If you have asked them to hang up towels
after showering but they wind up
on the floor, the next day the kids can
"drip-dry." They'll learn quickly!

244

Make a list of morning tasks
that routinely need to be done
before breakfast,
and post it in a visible place
to eliminate stress
and have a smooth start to each day.

245

Remember that your child
can't be perfect.

246

When your child is competing
or performing, help her learn to admire
and express appreciation for the talent
of the other competitors
or performers. To be a good sport
is to respect the talent of others,
instead of running them down or blaming
them for our defeat.

247

Encourage boys (and girls, too)
to always put the lid
and the toilet seat down,
a tidy and considerate gesture,
by placing a yellow sticky note
with a reminder message on the wall
if they keep forgetting.

248

Make it a family tradition to say only
positive remarks about the food served
at your table. When adults compliment the
food regularly, children tend to follow suit.

249

Avoid paying your children for chores
that are a function of being part of the
family (cleaning their rooms, taking care
of their own messes). Instead, offer them
a chance to earn extra money
for doing chores beyond their daily duties.

250

Every Christmas
ask your child to select one toy
he has received and donate it
to a family or children's shelter.
One twenty-something man I know said,
"I didn't always want
to give up a favorite toy,
but now I realize how this taught me
compassion, and I donate my time
to the city rescue mission."

251

To teach young children
to consistently put
their seat belt on before the car starts,
keep a stack of nickels
in the front seat.
Each child who gets the seat belt
on before the car
is in "drive" gets a nickel.

252

"Take a hammer
and share with your child,
'In life, you have a choice
in how you "pick up" or handle
what happens to you.
You can choose to pick up things
with the good handle
(demonstrate with right end)
or the bad handle
(wrong end of hammer).'
Have her think
of examples of picking up things
with the good handle."
—STEVE LAMB

253

Hold your child accountable for chores.
If he fails to do a required task,
withhold a privilege,
such as a scheduled fun activity
or TV program,
until the work is done.

254

Don't allow your child
to use the excuse "School is boring"
to get out of work.
Encourage her
to do her best work
even if the class is boring.
At the same time
you can confer with the teacher
about ways to challenge
her at home and school.

255

Have a "Dress Up Dinner"
occasionally where you serve
on china and crystal
and have cloth napkins:
Show how to set a pretty table,
where to put the napkin,
and practice using manners.

256

"When my father looked over the quarts
of huckleberries we children had picked
and he planned to sell,
he would pile on more berries so
that the baskets were well-rounded.
I have always remembered this lesson
on giving more than is actually required."
—Anna Belle Laughbaum

257

When your child does something wrong,
encourage her to say, "I was wrong;
will you forgive me?" Model it and she'll
be more likely to do the same.

258

To discourage complaints about the food,
put a jar on the table. Anyone who
complains has to put in a quarter,
which will later be given to a charity
that feeds the hungry.

259

"Man must work.
That is certain as the sun.
But he may work grudgingly
or he may work gratefully;
he may work as a man,
or he may work as a machine.
There is no work so rude,
that he may not exalt it;
no work so impassive,
that he may not breathe a soul into it;
no work so dull,
that he may not enliven it."
—HENRY GILES

260

Every year on the last day of school,
provide a scrapbook
for your child to arrange
her best schoolwork, report cards,
awards, programs from events
she participated in,
pictures of teachers and friends.

261

For jobs that are unpleasant,
rotate the tasks
among family members,
instead of dumping the distasteful
work on the children.
If you don't like to scrub the bathroom
or clean the refrigerator,
your children
will probably dislike it, too!

262

"Students do better in class if their parents
encourage open discussion at home.
Reason: Children need practice
in expressing their thoughts before they
can feel comfortable doing so
outside the home. When parents show
respect for their opinions,
children become unafraid to submit
original and independent ideas rather
than waiting to agree with the 'herd.'"
—DR. DELORES CURRAN

263

Model effective work attitudes
(enthusiasm, determination to finish
the job, and so on) and work habits
(diligence, etc.) as you and your child
undertake and complete a chore together.

264

Two factors that carry far more weight
and impact than our words of advice
and instruction to our kids are our own
behavior and the emotional bonding
that develops between us and our children.

265

When a child or teen works in a vacuum
with no one around him caring whether
he excels or flounders in school,
studying can become a dry, empty task.
Your support and positive comments
are greatly needed to help your student
exert a consistent effort.

266

"A child with an IQ of 95 who is respectful, responsible, and resourceful is *a far better student* than a child with an IQ of 165 who is deficient in those traits."
—JOHN ROSEMOND

267

"Don't put off until tomorrow what you can do today; tomorrow never comes." Don't sit around and talk about what you are going to do—*do it!*

268

Suggest your child write a note of encouragement to: ▶ a friend who is going through a difficult time; ▶ someone who is ill or is recovering from an accident; ▶ someone who works hard to make things run smoothly and is rarely noticed (a school or church janitor or a librarian).

269

"Reflect upon
your present blessings—
of which every man has many—
not on your past misfortunes,
of which all men have some."
—CHARLES DICKENS

———◆———

270

Have your child
help select a small gift
for the hostess
(scented soap, potpourri,
or homemade banana bread)
when spending a weekend or longer
at a friend's home.
With a thank-you card
she has signed,
she can give the gift
upon arriving or leaving
to show her appreciation.

271

Play "Gossip" to demonstrate
what happens when critical or negative
stories about someone are passed on
to others. In a circle, the leader whispers
a fictitious two- or three-sentence tale
to the player to his right.
That player whispers what he heard
to the next person,
and on around the circle. The last person
says aloud what he heard, which is usually
quite different from the original story!

272

"We cannot do evil to others without
doing it to ourselves."
—JOSEPH FRANCOIS E. DESMAHIS
Discuss this principle. Ask your child
to give examples of how she has witnessed
this (at school, in the news,
or in literature).

273

When rallying your children
to help clean
before company comes,
put on peppy music . . . dance a little . . .
whistle while you work.
This teaches kids
to make the best
of their responsibility.

———◆———

274

"The great—whether they be . . . senators,
famous authors or television arts,
explorers or scientists—
often suffer keenly from the insulation
of their greatness. . . .
The publicity manufactured
to build them up does not warm their
hearts. What they crave
is the spontaneous, human,
affectionate appreciation
of the people they are trying to please."
—DAVID DUNN

275

Suggest your child
write a note to a man or woman
in the public eye.
Her word of appreciation
or commendation can strengthen
or encourage some person
at a critical hour in his or her life.

———◆———

276

Learning to laugh at yourself
will encourage
an atmosphere of humor
at home. Dr. Smiley Blanton,
eminent psychiatrist, once said,
"I've seldom been called on to help
a person who had a sense
of the ridiculous,
and I've never had
to treat anyone who could really
laugh at himself."

277

We communicate
the value of family
by setting aside
time to be together—
to play a game,
to enjoy meals and conversation
regularly, to be involved
in projects or hobbies together.

278

Rhymes are a good way
to transfer values to your child.
To encourage finishing jobs at school
or home, put up a rhymed saying
and suggest your children memorize it:
"If a task is once begun,
Never leave it till it's done.
Be the labor great or small,
Do it well or not at all."

279

To encourage creativity, have your child
create a centerpiece of her favorite things.
During the evening meal,
talk about the items and ask her
to express what makes
these things special to her. Then praise
her for creating such a unique display.

280

Read a story each day
from William Bennett's *The Book of
Virtues* (New York: Simon & Schuster,
1993), an outstanding collection
of stories from great literature
and history that portray moral values
and integrity in an imaginative form.

281

Make it a goal to give your child
at least one positive statement
every day that affirms
his growing abilities, worth, or talents.

282

As a family,
decide on a candidate running
for political office whom you agree
could make a difference in your state
or community and volunteer
to campaign for him or her—
manning phones at headquarters
or canvassing the neighborhood
with flyers.

283

Encourage your older elementary child
or teen to teach
someone to read
through a local literacy program.

284

Avoid placing a television set in your
child's room or your own.

285

Talk about friendships with your child:
what kind of friends she wants,
how others evaluate us
by our friends and their behavior,
and how to be a good friend. Read
together *The Giving Tree*,
Shel Silverstein's book
about friendship and sharing.

286

During Thanksgiving or Christmas time,
look around to see who in your
community, church, or neighborhood
is needy, and as a family
select the special person.
Then set aside a portion of your family
holiday resources to make
an anonymous contribution
to that needy person's holiday.
In doing so, your child gets
to experience the joy of giving in secret.

287

Establish a "Child of the Week"
in your home
and the criteria for choosing.
This honor allows
one child to receive special privileges
during a week,
such as sitting in the front seat of the car,
staying up twenty minutes later
at bedtime,
or choosing a favorite dessert
one evening.

288

Show your own parents
honor and respect
by the way you speak to them,
the cards you send
for birthdays or anniversary,
and by helping them.

289

To reward good attitudes
in young children, make an effort to *catch
your kids showing a positive attitude*.
Give each one points
on a chalkboard under their names,
hung in a central location.
Each time you catch them in a genuine
act of kindness or displaying
a good attitude they get a point.
At the end of the week,
points are tallied, and rewards given:
for fifteen points,
a trip to an ice-cream store,
for twenty-five points, a new book, etc.

290

Let your child add sparkle
to his thank-you notes by
drawing a picture, including a photo
of him wearing or using the present,
or writing a short poem
expressing appreciation.

291

Wonderful classics
are often overlooked in schools today.
Your child can read these at home and see
solid values demonstrated: for example,
Heidi by Johanna Spyri (overcoming
hardships), *Lassie Come Home*
by Eric Knight (determination, dealing
with loss), *Charlotte's Web*
by E. B. White (friendship).

292

Decide with your child what percentage
of the money she earns or receives
should be saved,
and make sure she saves it consistently.

293

Provide a small light and worthwhile books
close by your child's bed.
Let him keep his lamp on an extra fifteen
to twenty minutes if he's reading.

294

Help your child discover
and use her talents
and gifts instead of hiding them.
An artistic child can help make flyers
and posters for community events.
A musically talented young person
can accompany a children's choir.
An athlete and encourager
can coach a Little League team.

295

Make clearly printed labels
to put on shelves and drawers in your
young child's room
to enable him to be organized
and know where to put things—
a "socks" label, "shorts,"
"sweat shirts and pants," "toys," etc.
For a pre-reader, you can draw a picture
or cut out a magazine photo
of the item for the label.

296

A mentor can be a big motivator
and good role model
for a young person.
If your daughter is interested in art
and design, find a graphic designer
she could help on Saturdays.
If your son is interested
in veterinary medicine,
perhaps he could assist a local vet
on school breaks.
Find a mentor in your teen's area
of strength or interest.

297

Encourage income-producing businesses
your young person initiates,
but help her *plan*: what to charge,
how to keep records, the duties
and follow-up involved in pet-sitting,
garden watering, etc. Having a business
can build many values: responsibility,
people skills, money-management skills.

298

Play "What If?" as a family.
Write out different situations
that would call
for an ethical decision—
one age-appropriate situation
on each index card.
(For middle-schoolers:
What if you saw
a classmate cheating
on a major test—what would you do?
The drug store clerk gives you
two dollars extra in change
and you realize it when you get home—
what would you do?)
Then shuffle the cards.
The first person picks a card,
reads the question,
and tells what he would do.
Others share
their point of view.
The group arrives
at what the right action
would be.

299

Tack a monthly calendar in your child's
room to record due dates
for school assignments, weekly meetings,
sports practices, and family birthdays.
The schedule will help her set goals
and complete projects
in several steps rather than doing things
at the last minute.

300

Good table manners show respect
and courtesy to other people. *Model* the
table manners you want your child
to learn. Demonstrate one at a time,
beginning with a few basics in the
preschool years, patiently reminding him
to: ►Wait to start eating until the hostess
has begun; ►chew food with your mouth
closed; ►never talk while chewing;
►keep elbows and arms off the table;
►when the meal is over, place folded
napkin beside plate, silverware on plate.

301

Practice caring for the environment
around your home and nearby parks
by planting flowers or grass
on bare spots to control erosion
and taking a sack on a walk to pick up litter.

302

Read a book to your child
that demonstrates the value of honesty
such as *The Tale of Peter Rabbit*
by Beatrix Potter
or *Pinocchio* by Carlo Lorenzini.

303

Find out what support
your child needs to succeed
in the classroom and provide it—
whether it's eyeglasses,
a lap-top computer,
or tutoring.

304

Have a "What Makes Me Happy?" time.
Around the breakfast or dinner table,
have each person name
what makes him happy—
what he loves to do for fun,
his favorite foods, his favorite people.
Go around the circle three times
as each person says one happy thing
as quickly as possible.

305

Display in a calligraphy, needlepoint,
or cross-stitch pattern the value
or character quality you are working on
with your child currently.

306

Teach your child: You're never a failure
until you give up. Losing a battle doesn't
mean you've lost the war. Tell about a time
you almost gave up but persevered
and overcame an obstacle.

307

"Share with your child
'The White Lie Test':
'When you lie to someone "for their own
good," will they thank you
for caring or feel betrayed
if they found out you lied?'"
—MICHAEL JOSEPHSON

308

Read aloud some of the great war
speeches and discuss the courage
they demonstrate, such as
Lincoln's "Gettysburg Address"
and Churchill's speech
in the last days of World War II.

309

Watch selected TV programs
with your child, and then talk about
what you viewed.

310

Don't let your child quit during a "slump"
while she's learning
to play an instrument.
If enthusiasm has waned
or she has a special hurdle to get over,
see her through that low point
(offer a change in music,
change in practice time, etc.).
Then after the recital
or accomplishment, sit down
and discuss the issue of taking lessons
and if she wants to continue.

311

With your child,
make a list of "wants" and "needs."
If he desires something that is a "want"
instead of a "need,"
encourage him to set a goal:
save his money for it, do extra jobs to raise
at least half the cost. Then match what
he makes to purchase the "want."

312

"Labor to keep alive in your breast
that little spark of celestial fire,
called Conscience."
—George Washington

313

When there is too much emphasis
on a student having
to make certain grades consistently,
cheating escalates
(it's already epidemic in American high
schools). Emphasize what your child
is learning, if she is being challenged,
if she is making progress
in her subjects and developing goals.

314

Help your child choose a few areas
in which he would like to work toward
excellence, rather than trying
to be number one in everything.

315

Creativity and curiosity,
initiative, perseverance,
and a burning interest—
many of these factors
have a bigger stake in determining
a person's success
than certain letter grades
on a report card.

316

Suggest that your young child
set small, realistic goals,
like "After I learn these five states
and capitals and finish my math sheet,
I'm going outside to play a while."
For a longer assignment,
have her use the calendar
to break down the task into steps
and place a sticker
on each step completed.

317

Prepare young children
for what is going to happen
and they will be more cooperative.
"The Gales are coming for dinner tonight."
"In fifteen minutes
we are leaving for the library;
soon you can start putting away your
Legos." Verbal cues reduce anxiety
and increase cooperation.

318

Day by day, give your child
snapshots of his strengths,
affirming the qualities you see
and you hope will grow:
"I love seeing how you cared
for the new kittens,"
"You really know how to rearrange
and turn a mess into a lovely place,"
or "That card you gave me
cheered me up. You really know how
to encourage someone."

319

Dreams and dedication
are a powerful combination.

320

Discuss a situation in which you were lied
to and how that affected you.
Ask your child to describe a situation
in which he was lied to. (How did he feel?
Did he trust the person any less after the
incident?) Talk about
the importance of honesty.

321

Encourage your child
to dream big dreams about a career,
mission, or quest,
and help her to plan
and pursue the dreams
in stages.

322

Identify what style
of learning your child has
and adapt the way
you deliver messages
and give instructions:
depending on whether he remembers
and does things best
from reading
(provide a list of what you
want him to do);
hearing (tape record instructions);
or moving (provide a Walkman
with taped instructions).

323

Humor oils
the wheels of family life
and helps to keep it running smoothly.
Find a humorous comic strip
to share with your child
and put on the refrigerator today.

324

Encourage your child
to reach out to classmates
who seem lonely
or who don't fit in, not just to make
friends with popular kids. One dad who
did this said his daughter befriended
a handicapped student
who was new at her school
and invited her home to play.
There the girl told the daughter
that she had thought
she'd never have a friend at school
and that she was the best friend
she'd ever had.

———◆———

325

A yellow sticky note
on your child or teen's bathroom mirror
is a good place to write
a quick thought for the day,
an inspiring verse,
or an encouraging word.

326

Make a video that records a grandparent's
or older relative's oral history.
To generate memories, ask questions like:
Can you tell me about your childhood
home? The people who lived there?
What was going on in the world/U.S.
at the time? What childhood
and school adventures do you recall?

327

"Love is a great beautifier."
—LOUISA MAY ALCOTT

328

Set aside an evening meal
to take the phone off the hook and have
each person share something
he learned or experienced that day,
tapping into your collective thoughts
and happenings.

329

If you are fortunate enough to live in the country and your children can help take care of horses, rabbits, and other animals, they develop a respect and appreciation for living things. If you live in the city, spend a day on a working farm watching and helping with the daily chores.

330

Invite a foreign exchange student to live with your family for a summer, semester, or year while he or she attends school.

331

Don't take over every time your child struggles with a challenge or difficult task. Our children are going to run up against problems, and we need to stand by them with support but not rescue. Encourage them to look for solutions, brainstorm together, and have them list possible strategies.

332

When your child has a negative attitude,
have an "Attitude Check."
It's a non-accusatory way to defuse
emotions, help her back off,
and check her own attitude.

333

Take advantage of "teachable moments"
to share your values and wisdom
with your child. A walk to the park,
viewing the night sky, or even baking
cookies can provide such an opportunity.

334

"We always had someone living with our
family—an aunt, a nephew, an exchange
student. It kept our family system an open
instead of a closed one, and our children
grew up conscious that they could care for
other people, offer a helping hand,
or even bring them home."
—PATTY JOHNSTON

335

Teach your child
that it's *okay to be different*;
in fact, it takes more character
to do what the crowd
is *not* doing
than to go along with
what the group decides.
Say, "Take a stand for what
you believe, even if that stand displeases
your peers or teachers,
and know that I will stand
behind you."

336

Show your love
by teaching your child something
at which you are skilled.
One dad gave his adolescent son
lessons in computer programming
and hooking into an Internet.
A mom gave her daughter gourmet
French cooking lessons.

337

When your child makes a statement
contrary to your values,
reason with him rather than overreacting.
Help him go through the thought
processes, and keep an open dialogue
about the issues and situations he faces.

338

Plan your own family sex education
curriculum to share with your child.

339

Suggest your child give coupons as gifts
for special occasions. Coupons contain
a promised service like
"This coupon entitles you to breakfast
in bed any Saturday of your choice in the
month of January. Love, Allison" or "Two
weeks of snow shoveling
and hot chocolate afterward,
Dad. Happy Birthday! Love, Brad."

340

Children see themselves in the mirror
of our facial expressions
as we look at them—
our smiles or frowns, our acceptance
or disapproval. Be aware of the looks
you give your child.
Do your smiles and eyes build up your
child or cause anxiety and insecurity?

341

Children with learning problems
need supportive parents
who know they are not lazy or stupid
and instead look for their strengths,
have high expectations,
and provide tutoring
or other help they need to succeed.
These kids need to know
they may have to work harder
than some classmates, but in the process,
they'll develop perseverance
that will be valuable for a lifetime.

342

Use a holiday chain to help your child
do caring deeds for others while counting
down the days until Christmas.
First cut some red and green construction
paper into one-by-eight inch strips.
On each strip write a simple holiday
activity like, "Invite a friend
to go see lights." "Make cookies
for neighbor and deliver." "Buy two pairs
of children's mittens and take to homeless
shelter." Glue the strips together
into links and have your child tear off
a link each day and do the activity.

343

Unexpected rewards have more positive,
longer-lasting impact than planned
rewards or bribes ("If you do this, I'll give
you this"). Surprise your child with,
"Hey, things are going well for you
at school and home—you've really been
putting out effort; let's celebrate!"

344

Encourage your child's developing
sense of patriotism
by watching a movie or video together
on the beginnings of the United States
and discussing the ideals and principles
on which our country was founded.

345

Discuss with your child the meaning
of the following, and talk about what new
habit you would each like to develop:
"Sow a thought, reap an act;
Sow an act, reap a habit;
Sow a habit, reap a character;
Sow a character, reap a destiny."
—ANONYMOUS

346

How would you act
each moment if you knew you were being
videotaped for a permanent record?

347

Pick some words
that describe character qualities
you want your child to develop
and together look them up
in the dictionary.
On a big piece of drawing paper,
have her write each word
and its definition
(and synonyms) and below
it draw a picture that illustrates
the character quality.

348

"Help your child or teen avoid
the 'I Deserve It' syndrome:
'Whatever I want, I need;
whatever I need, I deserve;
whatever I deserve, I have a right
to have—and I'll do whatever
it takes to get it.'"
—MICHAEL JOSEPHSON

349

Play board games
with your child and help him learn
to follow the rules and play fairly.
Toddlers and preschoolers
do not totally understand game rules,
but older kids can grasp
the concept and learn
to "play the game" according to the
instructions. Model the fact
that having fun, playing fairly,
and being a good sport
whether you win or lose
are more important than winning.

350

Remind your child to return promptly
T-shirts, toys, books,
and other things she borrows
from friends. Whenever she reorganizes
her room, have her make a stack
of borrowed items
and deliver them to the owners.

351

Make a list of ways you can conserve
energy and resources as a family.
Then set about to do them, such as:
▶ Start a neighborhood recycling program.
▶ Separate plastic and aluminum
from the rest of the garbage. ▶ Write on
both sides of paper. ▶ Give outgrown
clothes, books, and toys to charity.

352

"Concentration is the secret of success
in politics, in war, in trade; in short,
in all the management of human affairs."
—RALPH WALDO EMERSON

353

Give your child the gift of availability:
Even if you leave dishes in the sink
and laundry to be done tomorrow,
be there for the big moments and small,
daily moments in your child's life.

354

A child needs to learn to concentrate
on a project and focus intently
on a problem to solve it.
You can help him develop concentration:
▶ Turn off radio, television,
and other noise while he is working;
▶ supply a clean, uncluttered working
area; ▶ make a "Don't Disturb;
Genius at Work" sign for special work
times; ▶ focus on one assignment or task
at a time; ▶ provide a reward
for finishing the job—
a snack and break, a game time.

355

"I have a dream
that my four little children
will one day live in a nation
where they will not be judged
by the color of their skin,
but by the content of their character."
—MARTIN LUTHER KING

356

At mealtime discuss
these thought-provoking questions:
"If everyone did something,
would that make it a good thing?"
"Can you cheat a cheater
without becoming a cheater?"
"How honest do you have to be
when you know
it is going to hurt?"

———※———

357

Children aren't born with prejudice;
instead, they learn it while growing up
in their family and community.
By your example and instruction,
by friendships and attitude, encourage
your child to treat every person according
to his or her individual characteristics
and to respect everyone.

358

Frequently reaffirm the value
of *commitment* to each member
of your family, especially your children:
"We have a love that lasts. We'll always
stick together. We can solve problems,
and we won't give up on each other."

359

Help your child set goals and reach them
by setting realistic, but challenging goals;
writing down an "action plan"
for how each goal is going to be met;
reevaluating goals once a week or month.

360

Encourage your child to sit up straight
in class, listen well, maintain eye contact
with the teacher, show interest
with facial expressions and body language,
and sit close to the front of the room.

361

You can help develop
your child's speaking skills
by letting her speak for herself
when she is asked questions
and *not* cutting her off in the middle
of sentences or injecting
negative remarks.

———◆———

362

Show your child
good people skills, like how to greet
people by name, smile,
think the best of people,
and give them the benefit of the doubt.

———◆———

363

"The mind is its own place,
and in itself can make a Heaven of Hell,
a Hell of Heaven."
—JOHN MILTON

364

Remind your child that he can be about
as happy as he chooses to be.
When something difficult happens
(his team loses their sixth soccer game)
it can produce negative self-talk.
("We're terrible. I ought to quit.
Nothing ever turns out right.")
Talk through alternative statements he can
say to himself like:
"We lost this week but next time
we'll do better. We're in a hard league,
but I'll keep trying."

365

Remember, love covers
a multitude of sins and mistakes.
Pray for the love that covers,
that you will fall in love
with your children every day,
and to have eyes
that see the best in them.

Author

Cheri Fuller is an experienced educator who has taught at every level from elementary to college. She is the author of six previous books and numerous articles in *Family Circle, CHILD, Focus on the Family*, and others. She has also appeared on many television and radio programs, and is a popular speaker to parent groups and teacher seminars. She and her husband, Holmes, live in Oklahoma City with their three children.

Other books by Cheri Fuller, also available from Piñon Press: *Unlocking Your Child's Learning Potential*, *365 Ways to Help Your Child Learn and Achieve*, and *365 Ways to Build Your Child's Self-Esteem*.